Kiki
and
The Red Shoes

By Bess T. Chappas

Illustrated by Sandy Branam

Acknowlegements

Writing this book was a labor of love. It could not have come to fruition without the encouragement and support from family and friends. A special thanks to my friend, Virginia, who has been there from the very incipience of "Kiki", and to Susan, Sheri, and Melissa, my Thursday morning writers group.

Juvenile Fiction.
Recommended ages 5-10.
Summary: In 1939, a pair of red shoes from America, sent to a six-year-old girl in Athens, Greece, play a surprising role in her school program.

ISBN-13: 978-1-60131-012-5

Library of Congress Control Number: 2007930891

Copyright © 2007 by *Bess T Chappas*
Printed and bound in the United States of America
First printing 2007

To order additional copies, please go to:
www.SavannahStorySpinners.com

115 Bluebill Drive
Savannah, GA 31419
United States

All rights reserved. No part of this book may be reproduced or transmitted in any form or by any means, electronic or mechanical, including photocopying, recording or by an information storage and retrieval system – except by a reviewer who may quote brief passages in a review to be printed in a magazine, newspaper or on the Web – without permission in writing from the publisher.

This book was published with the assistance of the helpful folks at DragonPencil.

www.DragonPencil.com

*For my mother, Dora A. Turner,
my brother, Peter L. Turner,
and my aunt, the late Christina Legatos,
who shared this experience with me.*

Six-year-old Bess and her brother, Peter, (the real "Kiki" and "Yannie") along with Mama. Portrait made in Athens, Greece.

From left to right, Bess, Kay Turner Ducey, Peter, and Mama. Mentioned in the story is the fox fur around Mama's neck and the brown coat Peter is wearing. Picture was taken at the Zappion Gardens in Athens.

Kiki ran toward a small white house nestled on a narrow street in Athens, Greece. In the distance, the ivory columns of the Acropolis sparkled in the bright afternoon sun.

Clutched in her hand was a piece of paper.

"Mama, Mama," she called, as she rushed into the kitchen waving the paper. "The first graders are having a program at school and my teacher, Miss Maria, gave me a poem to say!"

"That is wonderful," smiled Mama. "You can wear your pink Easter dress. I think it still fits."

"But, I need new shoes," said Kiki, looking down at her worn sandals. Maybe Aunt Christina's box will come soon. Sometimes she sends shoes."

At the mention of Aunt Christina's box, Kiki's little brother, Yannie, came running into the kitchen. "Did Aunt Christina's box come today?" he asked. "I hope she sent us some toys and not just clothes."

Twice each year, a large box filled with stylish American clothes came to their little white house. Often, Aunt Christina sent books and small toys. Kiki and Yannie carefully examined every single item and daydreamed about the mysterious far away place called America.

Once, Aunt Christina sent something really strange. It was a long fur piece with a bushy tail and glass eyes. Mama said that it was something ladies wore around their neck like a scarf.

Kiki played dress-up with the furry scarf, but Yannie was afraid of its little beady glass eyes.

The next day at school, Kiki and her best friend, Sophia, practiced their poems by reading them to each other. "My mother is going to buy me a new dress and black patent leather shoes to wear to the program," bragged Sophia. Some of the other children said they were wearing traditional Greek costumes. Kiki didn't say anything. She wondered if she would have new shoes for the program.

Kiki soon memorized her poem and repeated it over and over again. Yannie ran outside to play when he heard her rehearsing. Even Mama was tired of hearing it, but Kiki wanted her poem to be perfect. When she thought of standing on the stage in front of strangers, her stomach would flutter.

Miss Maria explained to Kiki that her poem was an important one. It told how the Greek children of long ago met their teachers at night, with only the moon to guide them.

At that time, the Greeks were slaves of the Ottoman Turks and the children were not allowed to go to school or to church. Kiki, who loved her church and loved to read was glad she did not live way back then.

*T*wo weeks before the program, the long awaited box arrived from America. Kiki and Yannie watched wide-eyed as Mama pulled out dresses, hats, and jackets.

Kiki held her breath. Would there be shoes for her?

Out came a brown wool coat for Yannie. Some books and a small wooden train followed. Yannie yelled with joy.

Still no shoes for Kiki.

Finally, at the bottom was a small box. Could this be for her? Kiki opened the box and pulled out a pair of shiny, red patent leather shoes.

"Oh, how beautiful!" cried Kiki. " Now I have new shoes to wear to the program."

She quickly slipped them on, and they fit perfectly!

Attached was a note from Aunt Christina. "Dear Kiki," read Mama. "I hope you like your new shoes. I sent red ones because I remembered that red is your favorite color. Love, Aunt Christina."

The next day at school, Kiki told Sophia about the shiny, red shoes she would wear to the program with her pink dress.

"Red shoes! Kiki, they won't go with your pink dress," said Sophia. Kiki could hardly hold back the tears. Sophia was seven and she knew about such things.

The tears spilled out as soon as Kiki arrived home that afternoon. Between sobs, she explained the fashion mistake to Mama.

"What nonsense!" exclaimed Mama. "Who said red doesn't go with pink? That's ridiculous! Your aunt sent you lovely shoes, and you will wear them. Besides, you know we are saving our money to go to America to be with Papa. There is no extra money to buy another pair of shoes." She gave Kiki a stern look that meant the subject was closed.

Kiki did not say anything else. Mama had explained about the war in Europe. The year was 1939 and the war was coming closer and closer to Greece. Papa wanted them to sail to America as soon as school was out.

As the day of the program approached, Kiki almost forgot about the red shoes. She was afraid that she would not remember her poem.

"Don't worry, Kiki," said Mama. "You know your poem perfectly." But, Kiki was worried. The more she thought about being on that big stage, the more nervous she became.

At last, the day of the program arrived. On the way to school that morning, Kiki asked Mama to sit up front on the right side of the auditorium. "If I see you in front when the curtain opens, I won't be frightened." she said.

"All right," said Mama. "Yannie and I will sit in front where you can see us. Everything will be fine."

But everything was not fine. When Sophia saw Kiki's red shoes, she shook her head. Later, Kiki saw Sophia whispering to one of the other girls.

Kiki knew they were looking at her feet. Her shoes were so shiny, so bright, so RED!

To make matters worse, a few of the children did not come that day, so Miss Maria rearranged the children on the stage and Kiki ended up on the other side. "But, Miss Maria," protested Kiki, "I told Mama I would be on the right side of the stage."

"For heaven's sake, Kiki. What difference does it make? Just do as you are told."

Kiki moved to the other side of the stage. She was sure she would not be able to see Mama and Yannie when the curtain opened.

Suddenly, Kiki couldn't remember how her poem began. Mama would be so embarrassed. Her stomach began to hurt and she felt hot all over. She fought back the tears as the curtain slowly opened.

Kiki blinked as she looked out into the sea of faces. She couldn't believe it. There was Mama and Yannie right in front of her. How did they know she had changed sides? Mama and Yannie smiled and waved. Her stomach stopped hurting. She felt so much better.

When Miss Maria called her name, Kiki stepped out, took a deep breath, and began to recite her poem.

OH BRIGHT AND SHINING MOON,
LIGHT MY WAY TONIGHT.
HELP ME FIND MY WAY TO SCHOOL,
TO LEARN TO READ AND WRITE.
TO LISTEN TO THE WISDOM OLD,
AND HEAR THE WORD OF GOD BE TOLD.

When she finished, everyone in the audience clapped. Yannie clapped the loudest.

After the program, Kiki couldn't wait to ask, "How did you know I had changed sides on the stage? How did you know where to sit?"

"*It* was the red shoes!" cried Yannie. "We could see the shiny red shoes under the curtain, so we knew where you were standing."

Kiki breathed a silent thanks to Aunt Christina and the shiny red shoes. What a wonderful story she would have to tell Papa and Aunt Christina when she arrived in America!

Shining Moon

Oh bright and shining moon,
Light my way tonight.
Help me find my way to school,
To learn to read and write.
To listen to the wisdom old,
And hear the word of god be told.

Φεγγαρακι

Φεγγαρακι μου λαμβρο,
Φεγγε μου να περπατω.
Να πηγαινω στο σχολειο.
Να μαθαινω γραμματα,
Γραμματα σπουδαματα,
Του Θεου τα πραγματα.

Bess T. Chappas, born in Kalamas, Greece, immigrated to the U.S. with her family in 1939. Since retirement as a teacher and school media specialist, she spends her time as a professional storyteller and freelance writer. Bess has produced a story CD, entitled, *Savannah Ghosts and Other Stories*, available at cdbaby.com/cd/besstchappas. *Kiki and the Red Shoes* is her first children's book. A sequel, *Kiki and the Statue of Liberty*, is planned for next year.

Sandy Branam is an award winning artist in Savannah, Ga., where her drawings, paintings, and sculptures have been shown in several galleries and numerous exhibitions. She studied art at Berea College, Leeds University (England), and the University of Kentucky. She was also a teacher in Montessori schools. She and her husband of almost fifty years have two sons, four grandchildren, three parrots, three cats, and one dog.